PICKL

BEGINNERS:

Top Tips To Finally Master Everything You Need To Know About Playing Pickleball, Knowledge Of Kitchen And Dinks, and How To Score In Pickleball

Grant Dittman

Table of Contents

Introduction

Learning how to play pickleball is no difficult. You learn from someone who knows how to play. Optimally, it should be a certified pickleball instructor or registered pickleball teacher. These people are not just good pickleball players; they are actually trained to teach others how to play the game. In this book, I will tell you the best ways to practice and learn more between lessons, so you can learn how to play pickleball the right way quickly, without wasting a lot of time and money on things that won't help you improve your game.

Pickleball is a game similar to tennis and table tennis. There is a court to play on, much bigger than table tennis and smaller than a tennis court. You play with a hard paddle similar to table tennis, a net similar to tennis, and a wiffle ball that is plastic with holes in it. The main point of pickleball is to hit the ball over the net in a way so that the opponent cannot return it back, thereby winning a point. If it is your serve and the opponent fails to return your shot, you get a point. If not your serve and the opponent cannot return your shot, then it is side out and you get to serve. The game goes to 11 or 15. That is the basic idea but of course, there are more rules than that but I will not get into all the rules as this book assumes you know the basic rules and maybe have played a few games. What you really want to do is step up your game the quickest way possible.

Compared to tennis, pickleball success is driven more by ball placement capability and strategy than by strength and quickness. And, compared to tennis, pickleball success is driven more by eliminating errors than by trying to generate winners.

Let's get started.

Chapter 1: Basics of Pickleball

Pickleball is a paddle sport involving a whiffle ball and a tennis-style net played on a badminton-sized court.

Because of its simple rules and easiness of play, pickleball is appreciated by individuals of all ages and athletic abilities. The sport is popular at school gyms, fire stations, community centers, local parks, athletic clubs, and thousands of backyard sports courts since it is inexpensive, social, and healthy. Pickleball is a hybrid of tennis and badminton, and it has risen in popularity alongside sports like table tennis and racquetball. In recent years, tens of thousands more pickleball courts have been created, mostly in senior communities.

The USAPA and IFP (International Federation of Pickleball) publish the official rules for pickleball. Strict sorts will notice that the Official IFP Tournament Rules are available in the resources section at the conclusion of this book. If you just want the basics to get started, here are some standard rules: Basic Rules Keep in mind that the rules of pickleball are subject to change. They may differ depending on whether you're playing a fun backyard game or vying for the world title of the International Federation of Pickleball, but the following guidelines will apply in most cases.

• You can play doubles or singles. Doubles is the most common.

• The same size court is used regardless of player number: 44 feet long by 20 feet wide.

• The area 7 feet from the net is called a non-volley or volley-free area, or the kitchen. The remaining half is split into two regions: the right service area and left service area.

• The net should be 36 inches above the ground at each end and 34 inches high in the middle of the court.

• Pickleball may be played on a variety of surfaces and is suitable for both indoor and outdoor play. To allow the pickleball to rebound, the game must be played on a hard surface.

• A serve takes place behind the right service area to start the game. The server can't touch the baseline or step onto the court until after the pickleball has been hit with the paddle. Underhand serves must be delivered, with the paddle striking the ball below the waist of the server.

• The server's serves cross the court diagonally and must return to the other service area. The receiving team must allow the ball to bounce once before returning service, and the serving side must do so as well. After that, either player on either side may let the ball bounce once or hit it in the air before rebounding it.

• A player can't return a ball that has been hit by the other team if it hasn't bounced in the non-volley zone while standing in the non-volley zone.

• A point can only be earned by the serving side. When the non-serving team fails to return the ball, a point is scored.

• The serving team serves until it faults, alternating between right and left service areas. When the serving team fails, the non-serving (or "passing") team is assigned to serve.

• After a goal is scored, the game progresses until either one team has scored 11 points or both teams have scored

10 to tie. Some tournaments employ a 15-or 21-point scoring limit with the same 2-point margin requirement.

Pickleball Court Layout

A court is 20 feet wide by 44 feet long, just over half the length of a tennis court. That means each team's half of the pickleball court is only 22 feet long. If you haven't played, you may be thinking pickleball sounds like kid's play.

What makes pickleball so challenging is not the size of the court but the speed at which the ball comes back at you, and the fact that it doesn't bounce very high. Covering that small court is more difficult than it sounds

There are special rules for the kitchen area, the first 7 feet on each side of the net, officially called the non-volley zone. If you are standing in the kitchen, even if you have only one toe on the kitchen line, you may not hit the ball before it bounces. If you hit the ball in the air before a bounce, you lose.

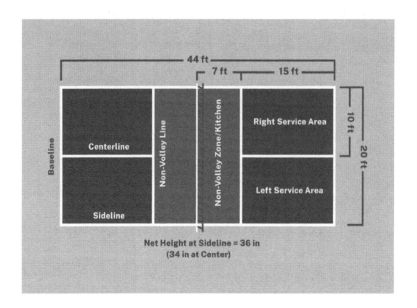

Equipment

If you are solely playing games that are quite casual, then equipment selection isn't much of an issue for you and you can buy equipment at whichever price range you feel most comfortable. If you are interested in becoming slightly more serious into pickleball, then these thoughts are for you.

Shoes

You really should play pickleball with a pair of court shoes, specifically. They will provide you with some ankle and arch support, they have good grip on the ground, and they don't leave scuff marks on the court. Also, some places require court shoes in order to play on their courts.

Paddle

Paddle selection is definitely a personal preference, but from all of the pickleball communities I have played with I feel a general consensus that the top paddle brands are Paddletek, Selkirk, and Onix. There are surely other brands that make good paddles, but these are the brands that I have seen the most.

As a general guide, basic paddles currently run anywhere under around $50, intermediate paddles around $80-$120, and expert paddles above $150. These ranges are not official by any means and there is gray area in the space between the ranges listed; however, this is my opinion based on what I see as of 2022. If you only want to play every once in a while as a social activity without practicing and trying to get better, then you can probably get away with purchasing paddles in the cheapest range. Try to look for cheap paddles that have good reviews.

Pickleballs

There are different balls used for indoor and outdoor play. Especially in recreational play, you might just have to use what you have, but the balls are designed to work better for the type of court you are on. Outdoor balls are harder, heavier, have smaller holes, have more holes (around 40), and travel faster. Indoor balls are softer, lighter, have bigger holes, have fewer holes (around 26), and don't bounce as high.

If you are just getting into pickleball, you might not care. Tournaments, however, do have requirements on which balls are used and so it is not absurd that people want to use specific brands.

Other Materials

Net

Athletic shorts

Sweatpants

Wicking apparel

T-shirts

Sneakers

Sunglasses

Hats

Visors

Sweatbands

Light jackets

Sweat shirts

Pickleball Winning Philosophy

To win at pickleball, you must have skills, mobility, and strategy. You need to have ball-striking and shot-making skills, the ability to move quickly to field shots, and a thorough understanding of strategy—where to be and where to hit the ball for every situation.

I believe another element separates the best from the rest: it's how you think. Many top players in a variety of sports such as golf, tennis, soccer, and basketball will even say that what separates the very best from the very good are not the skill sets. Instead, it's how the top players think.

It's how they go about winning. It's their method. It's how they work the point. It's their vision and plan, their long view, often thinking several shots ahead versus just reacting. I think this is the case in pickleball—that what separates the very good from the best is the difference between how they think.

Beginners don't play with a plan. Instead, they react. They try to win the rally with every shot they take. So they go for a fast serve, a fast return of serve...a fast every shot. In contrast, in advanced play, almost every shot following the return of serve will be a soft shot designed to land in the kitchen. An analogous beginner player in volleyball would seek to hit a winner from deep in the court rather than working to set up a spike.

The intermediate player may recognize the importance of getting fully forward quickly, but he or she will still try to do too much too quickly. When an intermediate player gets up to the line, he or she quickly goes for a risky shot.

The 5.0-rated player realizes that it's usually unwise to try to win the rally before getting fully forward. Once at the nonvolley zone (NVZ) line, the 5.0-rated player knows it's best to bide your time in a dinking exchange and wait patiently for a good opportunity before making an aggressive move.

Rally length and hit count data bear this out. In beginner play, most rallies end with five or fewer shots. Of course some of these rallies end quickly due to flubs and mis-hits. However, poor strategy is another contributor. Rallies involving the 3.5–4.0 skill level last a bit longer and have a few more hits, on average, than the beginner rallies do. Many of these rallies end due to poor shot choices and strategy. However, at the 5.0 skill level, not only do you see the skill and athleticism, but you also observe the patience, smart play, and withhold of attack until the right opportunity presents. Dinking exchanges can often go on for ten or more shots.

Ready Position

The ready position is the position players must assume before starting a point. There are some basic rules for the ready position:

1. All points start with a player in front of their court, in the ready position.

2. The player's paddle must be behind his or her head and touching his or her back.

3. Players' feet must remain on their court at all times during play (You may, however, step over your boundary line to retrieve a served ball).

4. Players' eyes must be focused on the ball being served.

5. Players may not block the opponent's view of the serving area.

6. It is important to follow this basic protocol because your movements during play may affect your opponent's ability to see and react to what you are doing. Improper movement can also cause confusion for spectators and interfere with their enjoyment of the game.

The Grip

Most coaches recommend, and most good players use, one grip for all shots: the Continental grip. Here's how to do it. With the paddle blade vertical (straight up and down), grip the handle as if gripping a hammer. If you were to hammer with the edge of your paddle, this is how you would grip the paddle. Some folks also call it a trigger grip. See Figure below.

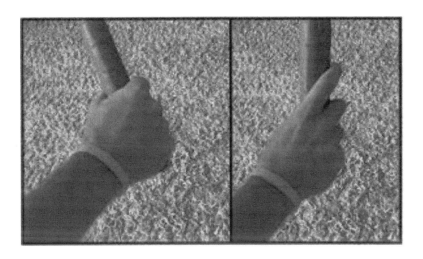

Hand position on paddle handle

Tennis players often switch grips between forehand and backhand ground stroke shots in order to use an optimal grip for each. Indeed, the Continental grip is a "compromise" grip, not perfect for forehand shots or for backhand shots, but is, instead, the best "one grip solution" for all shots. If you rotate your hand slightly clockwise (when looking at the butt of the paddle) to slightly improve forehand performance, you then degrade backhand performance, and vice-versa.

Most coaches advise to practice with and "work in" the Continental grip until you no longer feel any urge to change away from it. A good practice drill is to hit alternating forehand and backhand volleys against a practice wall. You obviously can't change the grip between hits. After a short period of getting used to it, you will realize that the Continental grip is the right way to go.

The neutral Continental grip gives natural, equal upward hits for backhand and forehand shots

Another advantage of the Continental grip is that it gives a natural upward hit for both backhand and forehand shots. Here's why. When playing correctly, you should be hitting the ball slightly in front of your body. Thus, your forearm is slightly angled up (toward your body). If your grip is correct, this should also angle the paddle up.

To the extent possible, the free hand (i.e., the non-paddle hand), should touch the paddle after every shot to improve steadiness, control, and paddle face aiming. If a right-handed player keeps his left hand on the paddle, his left hand knows where the center of the paddle is located and this helps when turning the shoulders to set up the aim point. Coach Mo suggests placing the tip of the middle finger of the left hand at the center of the paddle "sweet spot"

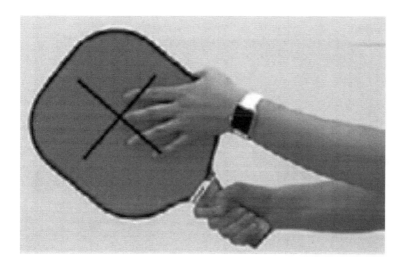

The paddle sweet spot

As far as grip pressure goes, you certainly do not need a death grip, but you can't allow the paddle to slip or have the face deflect in the event of an off-center hit. What's really important for about every shot in pickleball is that wrist action be eliminated. The wrist should stay firm.

Getting The Game Started

Pickleball is most often played as a doubles game. Twice the fun, someone to help you win, someone to blame when your team loses.

The big picture:

One person serves. A player on the other team returns the ball. Tit for tat.

Players keep hitting the ball back and forth across the net until a fault occurs. A fault is a screw up that stops play, like hitting out of bounds or hitting into the net.

A team can score only when they are serving. If the other team messes up, the serving team wins a point and keeps serving.

If the serving team screws up, neither team scores and the serve passes to the next player.

The first team to earn 11 points wins, provided that is at least 2 points more than the opponents. If the score reaches 11 to 10, the game goes on with the usual rules until one team wins by 2 points, or darkness is called. Most games are completed in about 10 minutes.

Easy peasie, but there are a few more complications:

There is a two-bounce rule. The serve must bounce once before it is returned, and the return of serve must also bounce once. Bounce. Bounce. One bounce per side.

After these first two bounces, a player may return the ball in the air – a volley shot – or may let the ball bounce once before returning it. Your choice every time, after all this is America!

For those who don't know a spatula from a tarantula, staying out of the kitchen is natural. But for others, it doesn't matter how many times we remind players of this rule, someone will violate it during every game. It's just too tempting to swat those higher balls in the air. I've thought about electrifying the kitchen line to make the point, but we don't have power outlets at our courts.

1-Find the availability of a pickleball or badminton court for a game.

Pickleball and badminton courts are identical in size, however a pickleball court's net is reduced to a height of 34 inches (86 cm). Find pickleball courts near you or at a gym that also has badminton and pickleball courts.

Pickleball courts can be found both indoors and outdoors.

Tip: If you're using a badminton court, ensure that the net is adjusted to the proper height for pickleball.

2 -Play singles or doubles with two or four players.

Pickleball can be played with two individuals competing against one another, referred to as singles play, or with two teams of two individuals competing against one another, referred to as doubles play. Singles and doubles matches are played on the same court, with the same number of faults required to lose their serve, and are frequently played to 11 points.

Pickleball is most frequently played in doubles.

3-Utilize a single pickleball and assign each player a pickleball paddle.

Pickleballs come in a variety of colors.

Scoring at Pickleball

This isn't about hooking up, although Pickleball is a pretty friendly sport. I'm referring to counting points and announcing scores during a game.

The scoring convention for doubles play has three numbers, and new players find this confusing. But it's easy as 3-2-1. Me first. The first number is my team's score. The second number is the other guys' score, and the third number says who is serving – the 1st or 2nd server. Me, you, who? A score of 3-2-1 means me - the serving team - has 3 points, you the receiving team has 2 points, and I'm the number 1 or 1st server for the serving team during this possession.

New players: don't obsess over how to say the correct score until you can actually score some points. It's not the first thing you need to learn.

Pickleball uses the "old" scoring system of badminton, which was in effect when pickleball was invented. Most newcomers to the game find the scoring system and the sequence of serving to be extremely confusing. It does take a while to learn how to keep score and how to switch servers and serving positions. Had the game been invented by folks who were not badminton players, I think the scoring system would use rally point scoring, in which the winner of a rally scores a point regardless of who serves. The modern badminton scoring system uses rally point scoring.

The pickleball scoring system operates as follows. A team can only score points when serving. Both members of each doubles team serve until faulting before the ball is turned over to the opposing team. This is called a Side Out. So each team has a first server and a second server.

Remember that the first serving team is only permitted one error before handing the ball over to the opponents at the start of each new game (a side out).

The game is played to 11 points, but a side must win by a margin of two points. It's not uncommon for many side outs to occur in a row with no points being earned.

Different Shots for Different Spots

There are several shots in the game you need to know:

Dink

A dink is a soft, short shot that goes over the net and lands in your opponents' kitchen. They will have to bend low to return it. A dinking contest is the meat of many points.

The whole idea behind the dink is to "strike" the ball so it drops into the opponents' NVZ AREA. You do not hit it over the net! **You push it over the net.** This is a huge difference in shot approach. Players who hit the ball over the net attempting to dink usually hit dinks that result in unforced errors or dinks that are very attackable. Players who hit their dinks usually take a back swing of 2' or more and this places far too much paddle power into the ball when you are only trying to hit the ball 5'-8'. A "straight-on-dink" has any where from 8'-14' to travel. A ball hit with a modified forehand or backhand back swing is going to be elevated over the net in an arc that is very attackable and probably will not drop into the opponents' NVZ. The solution is to push the ball back over the net. To push the ball with your forehand move/reach your paddle forward and in a "still"

or stopped paddle position with the paddle head pointing to the ground, push the paddle getting as close to the ball as possible through the ball with about a 6" to 12" follow through. There is no wrist movement in the dink shot. Your wrist is locked as you push the paddle forward. The paddle as it moves forward will

automatically lift the ball with enough height to clear the net.

The ball should go over the net and drop into the opposite NVZ. If you need an "aiming spot" try and hit the dink 1'-2' over the net so it drops within 1'-3' from the net on the opponents' side. This ball cannot be hit aggressively.

Please Note: The "straight ahead dink" requires no back swing to fall into the 8'-14' space/distance. However, if you dink the diagonal line connecting the two opposite diagonal corners of your kitchen and the opponents' kitchen, the distance is almost 24'5" and using a forehand or backhand 2'+ back swing is useful in having the ball travel that distance. The very top players in dinking these greater distances (up to 24') will "open" their paddle at 45 degrees and push through the ball allowing the 45

degree paddle angle to elevate and drop the ball onto the other side of the net into opponents' NVZ. It is not a slice but a push with an open faced paddle. The paddle travels in a straight path through the ball. It does not travel in a high to low swing which is a slice swing. That swing goes into the net. The very top players short-hop the ball or half-volley it. Catching the dink coming to you on the "short-hop" puts a little backspin on the ball and allows a little more directional control. It is, however, more difficult to accurately control the distance the ball travels. If you are dinking straight across from you and short hop the ball you run a high risk of the ball popping up in the air and getting attacked by your opponents. Short-hopping the ball to dink

diagonally has a much better margin-of-error as diagonally the ball stays/lands closer to the net and is not attackable. You can never over practice the dink shot! A great way to practice the dink shot is to play the dink game. This can be done as you are warming-up for your regular "club play". You play it as a regular game but the balls all have to be dinks or "dink volleys" and land into the opponents' NVZ. The server can either bounce the ball and serve it or hit a "regular" serve. All scoring and rotations are the same as a regular pickleball game. Do not underestimate the incredible benefits of this practice game.

Groundstroke

A groundstroke is a shot you hit after the ball has bounced. A volley is a shot you hit before it bounces.

A passing shot is like a line drive in baseball. It is an offensive shot that moves fast and in a straight line with no arc. It can be used to keep your opponent away from the net near the back of his court, a good place to stick him.

A lob shot travels in a high arc over your opponent's head and lands near her baseline. She will have to turn around to try for it, or just let it go and hope it is long.

Lobs can be a "rainbow" in your game but they usually result in a "downpour" of unforced errors. Three things can happen when you lob: (1) The lob can be hit too long and it goes out; (2) The lob can be hit too short and gets attacked by your opponents; and (3) The lob can be that "perfect" rainbow arc and fall onto the court non-returnable by your opponents. This "perfect" rainbow lob once achieved becomes the impetus for the next 20 lobs that fall into the other two classes of being too short and attacked by your opponent or too long and appreciated by your opponents. Just because there are three things that can happen to a lob does not mean you'll be successful 33% of the time. The vast majority of lobs are too long or too short. The "good" or "perfect" lob is seldom successful on the pickleball court. The very elite/top pickleball players will likely skip over this section as they do not lob essentially at all. Why? It's because they are younger, still in their athletic prime, and possess overheads that remind the players on the other side of the net why they shouldn't have lobbed. As we get older we still cover the same amount of court but it takes us longer to cover it. Our athletic "prime" is behind us.

We run slower and our reflexes diminish. The saving grace is knowing today's elite players will join our much larger group "tomorrow". In light of the fact that the vast majority of us realize the lob can be an effective weapon in our arsenal, we need to spend time examining the lob and the various aspects of its use and application. Just as there are offensive and defensive

overheads there are, also, offensive and defensive lobs. There are so many factors and elements involved in "lobbing" successfully that the actual execution of the shot is very difficult and high risk in nature. Since two of the three things that can happen to lobs are not conducive to winning, most people don't even try to put this shot in their game. Even if you fall into this group, understanding the lob in all of its intricacies may help you better defend against it.

Overhead shot

An overhead shot is one a player reaches high to hit. It is usually hit with a downward stroke and results in a slam the opponent will have trouble returning.

Overheads actually fall into the volley category since you are hitting a ball that hasn't bounced. It's very unlikely a ball/lob would be hit high enough that if allowed to bounce it would bounce high enough to become a "legitimate" overhead. Most overheads occur as a result of the opponents' lob strategies. In addition most lobs are offensive in nature and the shortness of the court limits the height of the lob. Defensive lobs can be hit as high as your opponent is able to hit it. A 20 foot high defensive lob allowed to bounce will bounce up roughly 8'8" which is high enough for an offensive overhead swing. This loses the volley status being allowed to bounce, but it's still an overhead swing or shot.

Important Point! There are probably more unforced errors hit from overheads than any other shot in pickleball. Not only is the shot difficult to hit well under "perfect conditions", once you calculate in the extenuating circumstances of sun, wind, and the mental "gymnastics" that occur during preparation for the overhead, the overhead can become a really difficult shot to execute. A very common mistake made by pickleball players at all levels of play is assuming that any ball hit in the eight feet or higher range should be attacked in an "end the point" swing. Overheads fall into two categories: (1) Offensive, and; (2) Defensive. You must be able to immediately classify the overhead required as offensive or defensive.

Your standing position on the court and the height and depth of the ball should lead to immediate recognition of your overhead as offensive or defensive.

Overhead "Rule of Thumb" – If the ball coming to your side is dropping in front of you or directly over your head it's an offensive overhead.

If the ball is behind you and you don't have time to get set under the ball, then it's clearly a defensive overhead.

Learn To Shuffle

As long as you are in the ready position, you can move. However, while moving around your backcourt it is important to learn how to play shuffleboard. Shuffleboard is an excellent way to learn how to move properly around your court because it requires you to use more finesse than power.

The basic shuffleboard rules are:

1. Players must keep their paddle behind their head and the ball underneath the paddle.

2. Players must remain in their ready position during all shuffleboard movements.

3. Players may not cross the boundary line to retrieve a ball.

4. Players may not stop until the ball hits the net after a rally or a bounce is made off your court.

5. Players must return to the ready position to continue play following play stops, including when serving and returning balls during rallies and while waiting for permission to serve again.

The most important part of serving is not how fast you can serve but how quickly you can get back to your court when your opponent has hit a good return. If you are trying to hit a super-fast return, take as much time as possible between each stroke to allow the ball to do what it needs to do on its way back. If you are trying to hit a flush return, the most important part is to get your racket back in position as soon as possible.

If your shot misses, then you will either have to pick up the ball or hit it again. Pickup is not a fast action but rather a calculated move to get the ball back into play and in the right place. The best way to get the ball back into play is to first make sure that you are over your court and on your side of the net. Then shuffleboard yourself over to where you want to put the ball.

Find a Practice Wall or Several Practice Walls

One of the first things you need is ball-striking skill, the ability to consistently get the hit and placement you want. To get anywhere in pickleball, you have to minimize flubs, mis-hits, and shots that go to the wrong place. Players at all levels will benefit much more from practice time than from playing time. This rule applies to almost all sports. While playing is more fun than practicing, playing is a very inefficient way to develop your game.

Here's an example in tennis: For each hour of court time, the average tennis player spends approximately seven minutes actually hitting the ball. The rest of the time is spent chasing balls in between points and getting set up for the next rally. In golf, the efficiency is worse. You'll hit about a hundred shots in a four-hour round of golf. If you practiced instead, you would hit at least ten times more shots.

Poor efficiency isn't the only issue. When playing versus when practicing, you don't get the chance to figure out how to correct your issues or how to perfect shots.

Because it's such a poor use of precious time, professional golfers essentially never play a round outside of their tournament schedule. Instead, they practice, which is a much better use of their time. Coaches involved with aspiring golf and tennis competitors usually specify at least a four-to-one ratio of practice time to playing time.

In the most ideal case, you have a coach, practice partners, a ball machine, a facility, and a schedule. But let's be real. Few people can afford all of the above. A less ideal but still great alternative is a practice wall or backboard.

In pickleball, you'll hit at least ten times more shots per hour using a practice wall (a backboard) than you will hit per hour when you are playing a game. Further, you can learn to steer the ball left and right, and you can learn how to volley, dink, serve, and hit many other shots. You can attach painter's tape to the wall to mark the top of the net location. I realize that many folks reading this will discard this advice without a second thought. Their reaction is the following: it's too boring; there's no time to do this; it's not the same as playing, so it's not going to help; or there's no wall available.

I urge you to not shut down on the recommendation of wall practice. I'll address some of the above issues:

It's too boring: Yes, it would be too boring if all you did was hit the same shot over and over. So you have to practice dink shots, forehand and backhand ground strokes, forehand and backhand volley shots, alternating forehand and backhand volley shots, spin shots, serves, drop shots, and lobs. There are a number of excellent YouTube videos, including some I made that show backboard wall drills for pickleball.

There's no time to do this: As the efficiency factor is so enormous (more than ten times for hits per hour than playing time), you need to spend, say, only fifteen minutes per day doing this to get a huge increase in skill. Because I have a concrete block wall in my garage and a brick exterior to my home, I can easily practice without traveling anywhere.

It's not the same as playing, so it's not going to help: True, you don't get exposed to all game situations, but in a real game, you don't get to repeat shots and focus on specific needs. Practice allows you to take a shot and push it to become better and better.

There's no wall available: I'm lucky. I have a block wall in my garage and a brick exterior on my house. But I also have more practice places. My church has a gymnasium with concrete block walls and so does my fitness club. If the gym is occupied, I hit against the exterior wall of my fitness club. The shopping center down the street from me also has a concrete wall exterior. Some tennis courts near my house have a practice backboard. So I have many places to practice. I think most folks can find one or more places that could serve as a practice wall. You can also practice indoors in your house using a NERF or GAMMA Revolution foam ball.

The benefits that come from using a practice wall will not come overnight. However, if you spend ten minutes per day using a wall to practice dinks, serves, drop shots, volleys, and so forth, I think, within six months, your game will experience a huge transformation. A good player should be able to hit a hundred or more consecutive volley shots against a wall without faulting.

Footwork Skills

Doubles pickleball position locations, movement directions, and the footwork patterns to get there are rather simple. The basic objective is to move your team fully forward as quickly as possible and then have your team stay fully forward and linked together. Once fully forward, your team moves laterally as necessary, staying linked, using shuffle steps. Usually, only a lob and perhaps an imminent smash should bring your team off the NVZ line.

Here are some basics.

Avoid Traveling Backwards

You should not travel backwards unless you must, and there are only a few legitimate circumstances that require traveling backwards. Most retreats stem from positioning and readiness errors. Here's what I see happen all the time in social/recreational play: players fail to get fully forward and instead position themselves in the middle of the service box. So, their feet are fully exposed to their opponents. In addition, these players are not compressed in a good, ready position that allows fielding shots coming low or toward their feet. So, when a shot comes anywhere near their feet, they attempt to scramble backwards. If they successfully return the shot, they only come forward to the same place where they were before. Thus the forward and back cycle can repeat. I've seen many falls result from the awkward forward and back retreat cycles.

To avoid backward travel remember these rules:

When on the serving team, stay behind the baseline with the server until the return of serve shot can be judged. A mistake is to move forward too early. If you move in too early or too far and the shot comes in deep, you have no choice but to retreat as the "double bounce rule" prohibits hitting a volley. As you will learn later, it's tough making a good third shot.

When on the return of serve team, the service returner should stay behind the baseline in the ready position until the serve can be judged. His or her partner should be fully forward at the NVZ line before the serve is made. Fully forward means the toes are no more than two inches away from the line. Once the return of serve is made, the service returner should quickly run forward and be fully forward at the NVZ line before the next shot—the third shot—comes across the net. About the only shots that should cause either of these players to back up or move away from the line are lob shots or imminent smashes. These at-the-line players must stay compressed in a basketball-like ready position to allow the fielding of shots coming toward their feet, to allow hitting low volleys, and to allow quick shuffle stepping or scrambling as necessary to reach shots.

When on the serving team and attempting to make the critical third shot drop shot into the kitchen, transfer your weight forward during the hit, quickly assess the quality of your shot, and, if it's good (not attackable), you and your partner need to scramble forward making as much forward progress as possible, hopefully getting established at the NVZ line. If you can't get fully forward before your opponent hits the ball, stop, split step, and get compressed at the moment your opponent touches the ball. Unless a great opportunity presents, continue the drop shot and scramble sequence until you can get your team fully forward. A common mistake is to hit a great third shot but not fully utilize the opportunity to quickly move forward. Top players can usually get fully forward to the NVZ line if they make a good third shot drop.

Whenever you are stopped in "no man's land," you need to be compressed and lowered so that you can hit low volleys or half volleys rather than having to back up. This is a key skill to practice and you can use a practice wall to do it. Here's how. Get compressed and lowered and hit shots at the wall that will rebound toward your feet. If you can volley it back, do so. Otherwise hit a half volley (i.e., a shot that is hit immediately after the ball bounces, well before it reaches the apex of its bounce).

Once all players are fully forward at the NVZ line, most movements will be lateral (sideways like a crab) only, with the desired style being a side shuffle step. Any shot coming toward your feet should be volleyed back rather than allowing a bounce. The top players stay tightly pinned to the line during typical dinking and volley exchanges.

Notice that the footwork, especially for the service return team, is really easy. One member of this team should already have both toes pinned to the NVZ line. All the service return player has to do is return the serve, with a semi-lob if necessary, and run forward to get both feet pinned to the line before the third shot comes across the net. From this point, mostly side shuffles during the dinking game are required.

Forward Movements

If you only need to go a short distance forward, use a forward shuffle (gallop) step. You might use such a step when making a slight adjustment forward when receiving a serve. If you need to get somewhere fast, like getting to the net after returning a serve or getting forward following a third shot, run, but stop and split step if your opponent hits the ball before you get fully forward.

Backward Movements

Let's look at some common scenarios where you need to retreat.

Deep, small adjustment. Suppose you are just behind the baseline but the return of serve is coming really deep and fast. In such a case where a small movement is required, turn sideways to the ball (like a batter) and use a sideways shuffle to set up for the ground stroke.

Short, disguised offensive lob from the NVZ line. From this close range, a disguised, good lob will be past you in less than a second. Usually, all you can do is drop one foot back and then leap. If your reflexes are too slow for this, you will need to turn and run and hit the lob after it bounces.

A high, deep, defensive lob, but sure to be in bounds. Here is a case where you have time to set up. Turn sideways to the ball and do a side shuffle or side-cross-side step sequence to get behind the ball. This is the way a quarterback in football turns and "drops back."

A deep lob that might go out of bounds. Let's say you are at the net and you get surprised by a deep lob. Your partner yells "bounce it," as it might go out of bounds. In such a case, will need to turn, run, and set up to play the bounced ball if it bounces in bounds.

Backing out of the kitchen. Many players avoid ever stepping into the kitchen. So long as the ball bounces, a step into the kitchen could allow you to make a better shot. However, when you do step in, do so with one foot only and then push off of this foot to re-establish yourself outside of the kitchen.

An imminent close-range smash. Let's say you or your partner just made a terrible offensive lob from the NVZ line, giving your fully forward opponent an easy overhead smash shot. You've got a big problem and there's no good solution. Fit and fast players may be able to get back a few steps and hope to make a block. If there's no time to move, get your paddle set to block and hope for a miracle.

Staying Linked to Your Partner

Beginner pickleball players usually seek to defend their side of the court only. The thinking is "this is my side and that is your side. I'll look after my side and you look after your side." Going along with this is the feeling that, "I can't give up defending my side to move over and help you. If I do, I risk having a shot come back to my side that I can't cover." Such a defense gets picked apart quickly by good players who will angle a shot to draw an opponent to the side and then hit the next shot down the middle.

Advanced players don't think like this at all. Instead, they are passionate about helping out whoever is closest to the ball by ensuring that the opponent cannot make a "down-the-middle" shot. In order to protect against the deadly down-the-middle shot, smart teammates stay tightly linked together, moving forward and back together and moving side to side together. The two teammates seek to form a wall that is parallel to the net and that moves in relation to the position of the ball. Communications like "go," "come up," and "get back" are helpful.

When the ball is near your teammate's sideline, he will need to cover the line and you will need to slide over to prevent the down-the-middle shot. Likewise, when the ball is near your sideline, you will need to cover the line and your partner will need to slide over to prevent the down-the-middle shot. When the down-the-middle shot is successful, the coverage fault is usually not from the person covering the line, but from his or her partner.

When tightly linked together forming a wall, the teammates will indeed leave part of the court uncovered. When dinking or whenever the ball is moving slow, this is not a problem because the wall can slide with enough time to cover sideline-to-sideline shots. However, if your opponent receives a volley opportunity, he might be able to send a shot crosscourt to the open area that outraces the wall. Still, the highest percentage action is to protect against the down-the-middle shot even if it means a distant area will not be covered. See Figure 6-2. When fully forward, both teammates need to watch out for the down-the-middle shot, which might be cleverly disguised, thus taking away some of your time to react. Likewise, if you see the opponent wall break open, keep your cool, disguise your intent, and send a shot down the middle.

Practice the Correct Forehand and Backhand Strokes

Of course, the serve is made with an underhand stroke with the head of the paddle below the wrist. Bending your knees will help you make a linear paddle movement through the ball striking zone. I urge anybody who is having trouble with the serve to practice against a gymnasium wall. Use a strip of painter's tape to mark the location of the top of the net. You can also practice on an empty pickleball court.

A standard forehand or backhand ground stroke would typically be used for returning the serve. In pickleball and tennis, the techniques for ground strokes are essentially the same, but there are two differences. First, pickleball strokes need to be shorter and more compact than tennis strokes, because you need to "reset" more quickly. Second, in pickleball, the ball requires more lifting or more of an upward hit than in tennis. For a standard ground stroke, the action is as follows. First, get into position quickly so you don't have to reach to hit the ball. For a right-handed player hitting a forehand shot, the stance will be angled so the left shoulder and left foot lead and are toward the net. For a right-handed player hitting a backhand shot, the angling is opposite. The paddle stays near the player versus being poked out wide to the side. The backswing should occur well in advance of the forward swing. The paddle path goes from low to high and is very linear through the strike zone. When hitting a ground stroke from deep in the court, it's best to wait until the ball is descending before hitting.

Almost all movement comes from torso rotation and the arm hinging at the shoulder. Almost no paddle movement comes from wrist or elbow movement. Movement coming from the shoulder creates a huge radius and thus small paddle path curvature. Through the point of impact, a blocking action is approximated where the paddle movement attempts to follow the same path as the ball for a long distance versus quickly swinging off the ball path. Obviously, small radius swings, as would occur from flipping the wrist or snapping the elbow, require extreme timing precision and thus yield poor consistency. Many unforced errors are due to poor stroke technique. Above all else, think about lifting or scooping the ball from beneath while keeping the swing path rather linear and close to your body. See figures below.

The forehand ground stroke

The Backhand Ground Stroke

The backhand ground stroke

Close to your body and scoop the ball

Tennis-like power topspin strokes that attempt to come over the top of the ball usually lead to failure for several reasons: power and control work oppositely, and trying to come over the top is not the correct paddle path. You have to contact the ball below the equator, brushing up, not over.

Chapter 2: Understanding The Pickleball Serve

For some reason, many otherwise great players struggle with the serve. Once their confidence is shaken, the struggle worsens. I think if you follow the suggestions below, you can end any struggles you may have.

Serving is a Privilege, Make the Most of It

Your team can score points only when serving. Don't blow your serve. Beginning in 2021, there are no "let" serves or do-overs. If your serve touches the net then somehow lands in the correct section of the opponents' court, it's good and game on. It may have lost some of its spirit by brushing the top of the net, but it's playable. But, if your serve lands in the opponents' kitchen area or out of bounds, you just lost your team's chance to earn a point. Big mistake.

The same player keeps serving as long as his team keeps winning points. The server alternates serving from the right side and the left side of the court.

Develop a Pre-Serve Routine

All great golfers and tennis players have a pre-shot routine where they set up for success and for a smooth and continuous journey toward making the strike. If you watch the professional tennis players on the Tennis Channel you will see that the pre-serve routine is extremely consistent from serve to serve. The following is a suggested routine.

Set your feet. I use a stance that is roughly square to my opponent. However, many top players use other variations.

Focus and visualize the ball flight path

Bounce the ball a few times. Most tennis players do this.

Call the score, ensure your opponent is ready, and spot your target, for example, dead center of the service box. Talking or calling the score while serving can distract you and cause faults.

While holding the ball against the center of the paddle, visualize a ball flight path that provides a very generous clearance above the net. Rotate your wrist to the right (for a right-handed player) to enable having the paddle face aimed at (square to) the target flight path.

Draw the paddle back while attempting to keep the face from shifting left or right of the target.

Hold the ball from above and drop it as you swing the paddle forward, trying to keep the paddle face always pointing to the ball flight path.

Once you serve, make sure you quickly get back into ready position behind the baseline.

Like the tennis pros, try to avoid any hesitations or variance. If any interruption occurs, go back to Step 2 above. Usually when I have a service fault, I realize that I was not disciplined in following the routine.

Many players use a serve where they step across the baseline when serving. It is perfectly okay to step into this shot. If you do this, you should get back behind the baseline in time to judge the return of serve shot, which could come to you very deep. Neither member of the serving team should be inside the baseline until after the return of serve shot has been evaluated. It's nearly impossible to hit a great third shot if you are retreating while trying to hit it. It's much easier to travel into the court than to travel out.

Some of the service swing comes from the weight shift toward the lead foot or the stepping out, some of the movement comes from upper torso rotation, and some comes from the shoulder. The arm moves like a pendulum from the shoulder. The movement is very similar to a straight bowling ball release.

I see many social players use a very quick swatting action that uses wrist action. Though many folks are successful with this, I would never recommend it. Instead, I think it's best to minimize paddle face rotation and curving at the moment of impact. This can be achieved by reducing wrist and elbow action and letting the swing come from the torso and shoulder.

To some extent, you can "groove in" your routine in your home, even if you have no practice wall. Just go through the steps and pretend to make a strike. If you have access to a gymnasium or tennis practice wall, you can practice your serve using a wall. You can use easy-to-remove painter's tape to mark the top of an imaginary net and a target spot. Otherwise you can practice on an empty pickleball court.

Serving Territory

To serve, when you strike the ball both feet must be behind the baseline and in an area represented by an imaginary extension of the sidelines and the centerline of your court.

It's okay if your feet cross the baseline with your follow through after you connect with the ball. One more thing: at least one foot must be on the ground when you connect with the ball – that means no "Air Jordan."

Once you execute the traditional or drop serve correctly from your court – half the battle – it must clear the net and land in the diagonal quadrant of your opponents' court beyond their kitchen line.

If the ball lands in the opponents' kitchen or touches the kitchen line it is short and a fault. If it lands beyond the baseline or outside the center or sideline, you messed up.

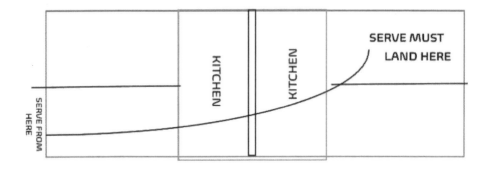

Types of Serves

Aiming the Paddle

Spot the target and aim the paddle face. Rotate the wrist and lock it in place.

The "swing" will come from the shoulder as the arm moves like a pendulum.

The back is bent.

Drop the ball from above and keep watching through contact. A mistake is to look up (or peek) too soon.

Step into the shot with the left foot.

The non-paddle hand drops the ball and then stays out for balance.

58

Contact

Keep the paddle face aimed at the target trajectory.

Drop the ball from above. Afterwards, the hand moves toward the target for balance.

Watch the ball make contact with the paddle.

Make a sound at the exact moment of contact to ensure you are watching the ball make contact.

You may step onto the court after contact. If you do step onto the court, get back behind the line before the return of serve is made.

The Drop Serve

For the drop serve, you hold the ball high in either hand and release it, letting it bounce anywhere on the ground. Then you swing your paddle and hit the ball to the proper quadrant of your opponent's court. That's it, no worries about anyone's waist or connecting below the wrist with an upward arc.

Your feet must stay behind the baseline when the ball is struck. The ball can actually bounce more than once, but geez it would be pretty low to the ground by then and you would be on your knees trying to hit it. You are not permitted to thrust the ball downward which would result in a higher bounce, nor toss it up in the air like a tennis serve. You must simply open your hand to release the ball letting gravity work, or you can place the ball on your paddle and simply tilt your paddle to let the ball roll off it for a drop. You must release the ball in a way that the receiver can see it. No slight of hand trick. If you don't like your drop, don't swing for a serve, simply pick it up and try again.

I don't see any particular advantage to this serve but some players say it saved their game. It would certainly work better with a new lively ball rather than with the slightly used balls we have. It may not be for me, but you should give it a try. Maybe you can find a way to turn it into a screaming slice winner.

You are permitted to use the traditional serve, or the drop serve at any time throughout your game, you don't need to own just one or the other.

Follow Through

Keep the paddle face on line. Think about pushing the ball along the desired trajectory line. Keep your head down until well after contact.

If you follow through completely and properly, you should be able to kiss your serving arm bicep at the end of the full follow through.

A Good Way to Learn How to Serve

A good way to minimize failure and immediately build confidence with serving is as follows. Instead of standing behind the baseline, stand very close to the net. See Figure 4-5. You might think this is so easy that it's ridiculous. However, I urge you to follow the system.

Use your complete pre-shot routine for every serve. Your aim point should be dead center of the service box. The ball flight path should clear the net by at least two feet. This gives you enough leeway for error.

Execute the serve and note the landing spot.

Repeat this until the ball is consistently landing in the middle of the box. Once you can get 10 in a row into the center of the box, move back a couple of feet.

Repeat the above until you can get 10 in a row into the center of the box, then move back a couple of feet.

Do not just hit the ball in the general direction of the service box. Instead, choose an exact target, visualize the exact trajectory you desire, and think about having the paddle face push the ball along the trajectory path.

You can also use a practice wall to develop your serving skill. Again, start close to ensure success, and then work further away.

For folks who are developing their skill my advice is this: focus on reliability. Your game will not be handicapped if you can consistently hit serves that land near the center of the box. Again, even at the very highest skill levels of pickleball, all that is necessary is a serve that does not fault and that can get about halfway back in the box. So, for developing players, I recommend aiming for the middle of the box and allowing at least several feet of clearance above the net.

Many pickleball teachers advise their students to practice serving deep or to backhands. My concern with this is that most attempts to hit targets away from the center of the box result in increased faults. In my opinion, of all the areas to work on in pickleball, working on getting a serve to land deeper than the center of the box should be low on the list.

The next time you go out to play, before each serve, spot the target (dead center of the box), and try to hit this target. Keep some mental notes on how well you did. I think you will find that hitting a target is more difficult than you think it is.

On your next outing, set a goal to have zero service faults. Count any faults that occur. Coach Mo drives the philosophy that you should not fault with your serve more than once per month.

Over your next several outings, develop your serving routine. It should always involve spotting the target and visualizing the ball flight, which should allow a generous clearance of the net and a wide margin for error.

Chapter 3: Pickleball Strategies and Techniques

Serve Deep

Get your serve as close to the opponent's baseline as possible without hitting out of bounds. You must serve the ball underhand, so don't worry if you can't hit it low and hard. It can he high and loopy. Whatever you can do to keep your opponent away from the net is your best strategy. If you can serve to your opponent's backhand and serve deep, even better. Most players have weak backhands and, if your serve is deep to the backhand, a weak backhand means a weak return, which gets you closer to the net to return the ball. Opening serve must land in the opponent's Right Service Area. Serve deep to opponent's backhand. This is your opening move.

Get Expert Help

Almost all great players in every sport have coaches. Certainly, this applies to tennis and golf. A good coach can likely spot and address your worst faults in just a couple of hours. A coach can help you bypass the trial-and-error process and get around beginner mistakes so you can quickly get to doing things right. I realize that coaches can be expensive and are not always available. In the absence of a coach, you may have to read books, watch videos, and seek the advice of the best players in your area.

Return Deep

Your opponents now have an advantage because one of them is already at the net. You and your partner must stay back because the rules state that your opponent's return must bounce before you can hit it. Your opponents have strategy options. What will they choose? If they return it deep, you can also return deep, or lob it over them, since at least one will be at the net. Once you make your return shot, you need to get to the net as soon as possible.

Get to the net first

Your ultimate strategy is getting to the net before your opponents. Statistics show this is where winning shots take place. One of your opponents is already at the net (see schematic), but if you return a lob over his head, you may be able to get him to retreat. In Pickleball, it is easier to take a ball out of the air than to hit it off the bounce because the type of ball that is used barely bounces up from the court. Besides, letting a ball bounce, gives your opponents more time to get to the net before you.

Practice/Drills

Once your coach shows you what to do, you need to practice it. This rule applies to almost all sports. Especially in tennis and golf, the pros use their precious time not to play a game, but rather to practice shots and perform drills. Whether in tennis, golf, or pickleball, to improve shot-making skills, you must perform the same shot repeatedly. I'm not going to go over all the procedures for the various drills.

Angle the Volley

This is a shot you can practice either off a backboard or by just tossing the ball high. Practice both forehand and backhand volleys. You won't have time in the actual game to switch your grip, so a modified grip is best. (Imagine shaking hands with the paddle. The V shape between your thumb and forefinger should be aligned with the side of the paddle.) If that isn't working, turn your grip counterclockwise until you can switch easily between forehand and backhand volleys.

Perfect the Lob

There is only one way to learn to lob and that is to practice. You can lob a ball that has bounced or you can lob a ball out of the air. Practice both ways. Bounce the ball and then bend your knees and lift the ball in an upward stroke. Bending your knees is really important. You want the ball over your opponents head while still in bounds and getting your knees bent will give you the lift you need.

Practice the Spin

The forehand spin shot is called topspin. This shot is made by turning the paddle at an angle and slicing the paddle downward as you hit the ball. You can make a spin shot in either forehand or backhand position. To use a backhand spin, you slice the paddle upward. A spin shot is hard to return because when the ball bounces it spins away or it never actually bounces up--it just dies.

Hug the Center Line

If your opponent beats you with one shot, that shot is probably going to be down the middle between you and your partner. Decide between yourselves who is going to hug that center line. You both can't do it. Since you are changing sides all the time with Pickleball, you might just decide whoever is in the left (odd) court (assuming you are both right-handed) will cover that center line.

Compete

One of the best ways to move from being good to being great is to compete in tournaments or league play. Likely, nothing will improve your game more than the decision to begin competing. Competing is a good way to measure where you stand and how much you are improving.

For most folks, their attitude toward competing is, "I'll get clobbered. So why do it?" Most tournaments have beginner, intermediate, and advanced brackets. For me, the most important goal of competing is not to win a prize but to get better. You become a better player by playing better players. You learn from them—both what to do and not do.

Dinking Techniques and Strategies

The better players in Pickleball know how to "dink" the ball so that it barely crosses the net and falls in the Non-Volley Zone commonly called the "kitchen." They may, in fact, be so skilled that they can have the ball actually graze the top of the net and then die on the other side. You can practice this skill. Bounce the ball and bending your knees get the paddle under the ball. Lift up on the paddle and aim for the net. You will need a lot of practice with this shot til you get the feel of it.

The dinking phase only occurs among players who understand that it's better to postpone aggression and scoring attempts until they are fully forward. These players must also possess skills such as the third shot drop that allow getting forward. Smart players know it's unwise to start a fastball fight with opponents who have a superior court position.

Suppose all four players are fully forward at the NVZ line. What type of shots do you use now? Typically you use the dink shot. Why use the dink shot? You should dink because you usually have no better options. When all four players are at the line and properly positioned, until the ball gets high or a hole in the offense occurs, the dink is usually the smartest or highest percentage action available. Here's why. When dinking, the ball will only bounce about 16 inches high, which is less than half the height of the net.

So, when your opponent hits an unattackable dink to you, you have these choices:

1. Hit the ball hard. Here's the problem. If it clears the net, it will likely fly out of bounds. A smart and skilled net player will let such shots fly out of bounds. To be successful with such a shot, the shot needs to hit your opponent or defeat his or her reaction time.

2. Hit the ball hard, but such that it will stay in bounds. Here's the problem. You have just given your opponent a great volley opportunity. He now has the ball above the net. To be successful with such a shot, it needs to go through a hole in the offense or defeat reaction time.

3. Hit an Offensive Lob. Here's the problem. Unless you have good skill with such shots, or poor lob handling opponents, you will likely lose more points than you will gain from them. Only when you have the combination of a good lobber and a poor lob handler does lobbying result in high percentage play.

4. **Dink the ball**. This is usually the smartest thing to do until somebody pops the ball up.

Once you get fully forward, try to keep your toes pinned to the line, (only an inch or two behind the line). If your partner is receiving the serve, go ahead and get both feet pinned in place. You can twist your upper body to watch whether the serve is in or out. Keep a wide stance, feet at least shoulder width apart, as this allows the fastest sideways shuffling. Getting your feet in place early and when you have a chance allows you to avoid looking at your feet when you should be watching the ball.

Avoid stepping back if a ball is headed toward your feet. If you are properly compressed, low, and holding your paddle well in front of your body, you can volley such shots headed toward your feet versus letting them bounce. So, when you have a choice between hitting the ball in the air (volleying) or after the bounce, reach and volley the shot, as fewer bad things can happen if you do. If you let such a ball bounce, it could take an unpredictable bounce or land in a tough spot beside you or behind you. Making a volley shot is easier than digging the ball with a half volley. Also, volleying the ball takes time away from your opponents.

No matter what shot you are hitting in pickleball—a dink, a smash, a volley, a groundstroke—you should seek to hit the ball well out in front of your body. If you let the ball get beside you, you give up angles and your opponent can better predict where your shot will go.

As the ball moves left and right, your team "wall" needs to stay tightly linked, sliding left and right in relation to the position of the ball. Try to preserve your ready position base as much as possible, so use side shuffle steps, if you are able, when moving laterally along the NVZ line. Less mobile players may not possess the speed and agility required for the shuffle step. So, less mobile players may need to use a crossover step, especially to reach wide shots. Crossover steps are not ideal, but they work fine so long as you can keep the ball slow, low, and in the kitchen so that you can uncross and get back in position for the next shot.

Movement along the NVZ line is essential. However, good dinkers stay tight on the NVZ line and don't dance around or move their feet unnecessarily.

To be good at dinking, you must be able to hit the ball when it's very low, barely off the ground. Your opponent will often aim to have the ball land right at your feet. You must be able to hit low volleys and half volleys. Great players bend their knees, meet the ball low, and stay low through contact.

You can use a wall or a practice partner to gain skill at dinking. If you use a wall, try to make the shots rebound so that they come at your feet. Handle these without backing up by making low volleys or half volleys. You will find that you can't do this drill very well unless you are compressed and low.

If you need to step into the kitchen, if possible, do so with one foot only (a lunge) and then push off of it to get reestablished behind the line. By the way, if you step into the kitchen, avoid hitting the near opponent. If you err and get the ball too high, he could hit the ball back to you before you have both feet reestablished behind the NVZ line, causing a fault on your part.

When you are involved in dinking, you must stay compressed and low, leaning forward, and on your toes. It helps even more to split step or adjust, if only slightly, each time your opponent touches the ball. You will need the agility, because sharply angled crosscourt dink shots and disguised "misdirection" shots can outrace you if you are not ready. When I am at the line and facing an opponent at the line and I see him standing straight up and flatfooted (therefore, glued in place), I can usually win the rally with just one dink. I use a misdirection shot to place the ball near a sideline.

You must stay linked to your partner, shifting the wall laterally with each lateral shift of the ball position. This can be tiring, but it's necessary. In a crosscourt dinking exchange, the wall should slide back and forth. A savvy opponent will look for a break in the link that creates a hole.

Chapter 4: Mistakes you should avoid in Pickleball

Trying to hit a winner rather than trying to keep the ball in play.

Hitting a sharp crosscourt winner brings tremendous joy, but for most players, attempts at such shots cause more lost points than gained points. If you simply commit to hitting unattackable dinks that clear the net by a foot, you will win more dinking battles than by going for aggressive placements. Often, when involved in a crosscourt dinking exchange, an aggressive player tries to go closer and closer to a sideline, eventually going out of bounds wide.

No Follow Through

The follow through ensures you've hit the ball in the direction you want with the power you want and the spin you've intended. By not following through you lose direction, control, spin effectiveness intended, and power planned. From a kinesthesiology view point you, also, stop the natural movement of the arm/swing in an unnatural way which can lead to possible injuries.

Trying to "kiss the tape."

Developing players, as they get better, often start trying to lower their shots too much, "kissing the tape" at the top of the net. This is not smart, as any slight mis-hit will dump the shot into the net.

Not Being Able To Modify Or Change

Not being "able" to modify or change your game strategy fortunately is not a life sentence without parole. It's unfortunate because it is avoidable. You should have a good idea of your opponents' assets and liabilities. You then play/attack the liabilities. When that doesn't work you need to have or come up with Plan B when Plan A isn't working. Plan B can include:

1. The player you are returning serve to

2. The **depth** of your shots

3. The **variety** of your shots

4. The **pace** of your shots

5. Go for **more angles** if the middle game isn't working

6. Maybe you need to use stacking yourselves

7. You might need to slow down or speed up the pace of the game.

8. Change your focus from defense TO offense or offense TO defense.

NOTE: You should only modify or change your tactics/strategy if you have the ability to execute the different tactics you decide to use/employ. If Plan B isn't working, go back to the game/strategy shots you and your partner are best at doing and just know you've given it your best shot. Don't forget to use "scouting" and/or pre-game warm-ups as a time to "evaluate" your opponents. If your opponents are the type who want to warm each other up before the match then you need to have done some "scouting".

Not staying low and compressed.

You may think you can lower in time to return a shot headed toward your feet. You cannot. You must already be compressed. A shot to the feet of a net man who is standing tall is almost certainly a winner.

Balls Hitting Net And Dropping Straight Downward

The error here is thinking you can reach/lunge forward and hit the ball straight/ up over the net in front of you. This will always end with you hitting the ball into the net. You can't get under the ball and hitting the back side of the ball won't work.

Solution: You have to hit the ball on the side of the ball hitting it parallel to the net to the opponents' diagonal NVZ sideline.

Even then the ball has to bounce at least three inches from your net side to have even a remote chance of the great save.

DRILL: Have practice partner standing at the net with the ball pushed down on net "fractionally" on your side. You stand at your NVZ-Line and when your practice partner lets go of the ball step in and return it from the side as explained above. Repeat from both ends of the net and across the 20 foot width of your NVZ-Line. Then let your practice partner have the same fun!

Not Being Patient

If you want to enjoy the "fruit" of the pickleball point/rally don't pick it before it's ripe! All of us have, at the least, a little impatience in us! Some of us have a lot of impatience in us. Being patient means we are waiting for something to happen or occur in the near or distant future. It's probably something we want to happen. That silly little pickleball point we are playing will hopefully result in our winning the point/rally. In the over all "scheme of life" that single pickleball point all of a sudden becomes really important and we can't wait to grab it. Being patient means you know that time is elapsing between this moment and the "thing worth being patient for". Once the urge for immediate gratification takes over, there are physiological changes that occur including our over-stimulated muscle responses and mental acuteness. You have now lost control albeit for a fraction of a second, resulting in a less effective result/response. We will simply call that an unforced error. "Things worth having are things worth waiting for"! Be patient, be focused, and enjoy the intervals of time and play in the process.

Crossing Through Courts During Play

I don't know which is worse: The player who runs/darts across the court during play which means s/he knows they shouldn't be doing that, or the player/person who unknowingly walks across the court/baseline during play. This common courtesy should be a part of every beginning instructional program and usually isn't.

Always ask permission to cross the court after play has stopped when in doubt. If you can "safely" and "politely" run/jog across the court after play has stopped, this is acceptable. However, far too many players walk and in many cases walk slowly across the court during a lull in the play resulting in the players having to wait to resume play. This is not acceptable!

Not Anticipating Speed/Pace

We've all gotten into the mental state of dink, dink, dink," or the opponents are going to hit a soft drop shot off our Return of Serve, etc. We get "consumed" by the rhythm of the ball going back and forth and anticipate that "beat" to continue and then realize the crescendo was delivered by our opponents and not us. Players need to change their "mental state" to think dink, expect smash, think dink, expect smash! Players need to expect/anticipate their Return of Serve will be "ripped" by the serving team and not a drop shot put softly into their NVZ. If you expect heat on every shot you have plenty of time to prepare and react to a slower hit ball. If you expect slow on every shot you have little or no time to react to fast. Do you ever wonder why the higher skilled players seem to have such great reflexes and quick hands all the time? Part of the reason is they do. However, the biggest part of their reflexes and quick hands is they are anticipating heat/pace every time and readjusting for slower balls. Most players anticipate normal paced balls and pay the consequences when they're wrong. You dink, expect smash, dink, expect smash, dink, expect smash!

Facing The Ball

The concept is incredibly simple: Both you and your partner, wherever you are on the court, must turn your body to directly face straight ahead where the ball is being returned by your opponent. If the ball is in the middle of the opponents' court, both you and your partner are slightly angled/turned to face the ball. If the ball is directly in front of you on your opponents' side, then your partner is turned/angled towards the ball as much as 45 degrees diagonally. Face the ball at all times when it's in your opponents' half-court.

Hitting Out-Balls

No one playing pickleball regardless of their skill-level has avoided this mistake/error. However, the common error element is that many players continue this problem repeatedly to the detriment of their team's successes. **Drill and Practice** as outlined in Section 2 on Hitting Out-Balls will help!

Not Getting To The Nvz-Line

If you are playing recreational pickleball then getting to the NVZ-Line is probably not a part of your game plan even though it should be. If you believe you are a competitive pickleball player and you are not getting to the NVZ-Line then guess what? You've overrated yourself! For the recreational players let me share one important fact with you. The highest percentage of injuries on a pickleball court occur in the area/spacing between the baseline and mid-court. If you always leave a twelve to fifteen feet distance to cover between you and the NVZ-Line you are inviting potential injury to yourself.

Kitchen Violations

The higher skill-level players have fewer incidences of the NVZ-Line violation due to their excellent footwork, balance, and court presence/awareness. If you have frequent NVZ/Kitchen violations try the following:

1. Stand six inches behind/from the NVZ-Line.

2. Spread your feet outside your shoulder width.

3. As if you were sitting on a chair, bend your knees.

If you still have frequent NVZ-Line violations doing these three things, don't back up even more from your NVZ-Line but simply spread your feet even wider with your knees bent.

Length Of Swing

You will seldom create unforced errors with a compact swing. This doesn't mean you don't take a back swing. At the NVZ-Line you never take a back swing! However, at the baseline you have to take a back swing because you are trying to hit the ball potentially 44-48 feet. Generally from the baseline, the length of the back swing is proportional to the speed of the ball coming towards you relative to ground strokes.

1. **The faster the ball is traveling towards you the shorter the back swing.** There's already power/energy in the ball coming to you so you don't have to generate that much power yourself.

2. **The slower the ball coming towards you the longer/greater the back swing** . You have to apply your own pace/energy because there's not much kinetic energy in the ball coming to you.

3. If you are "hitting"/pushing drop shots from the baseline you need that "good-ole" NVZ-Line control swing with little back swing.

Moving While Hitting

Next to hitting high risk/Low Percentage shots, moving while hitting the ball results in an exceptionally high number of unforced errors/common errors. You have to be stationary to have optimum time and control of your shots. Most moving-while-hitting-errors occur when players are trying to move towards their NVZ-Line/Kitchen. Try this: Hold your paddle out to your side and start jogging while trying to hold the paddle absolutely still. Observe how much the paddle moves even when you are trying to not move it. Moving forward and concentrating on the ball coming towards you and not on holding the paddle still causes even more paddle movement resulting in poorer timing and less control.

Not Enough Drill And Practice

If you are not improving and have remained at the same skill-level for an extended period of time, you are not drilling and practicing. If you are making a concerted effort to work on a specific skill or two and are not reaping the benefits of your drill and practice, then continue drilling and practicing because the learning process and moment of understanding and success is perhaps just another drill or practice session ahead. You do have to make sure that you are drilling and practicing with the correct techniques.

Better Return that Serve

Like the serve, the return of serve is a preliminary part of each rally. It's the second step leading to the third shot and the crux of the game.

Keeping the return of serve in play is just as important as landing a safe serve. Maybe more important. If you mess up your serve, you lose a chance to score but no one gets a point. If you mess up your return of serve, the other guys get a point. Ouch, that hurts.

That should tell you this is no time to go for a winner or try something tricky. Your job is simply to land a safe return, the deeper the better to keep your opponents in the back court on the defense.

Not Bending at the Knees

A new pickleball doesn't bounce very high. The gently used balls we usually play with have lost some of their resilience and bounce even lower. If you want to play lifetime pickleball, you must use your knees to bend for the low balls. Bending at the waist will eventually strain your back. It also changes your center of gravity, putting you at risk for a fall.

Conclusion

Thank you for reading this book on Pickleball. Pickleball is a great game of finesse. patience, and strategy. If you can master the basics and build from there, you will advance your game tremendously and rapidly. Remember, the goal is to always get to the kitchen line and control it to keep the advantage. Always be in the ready position at the kitchen line to maximize your ability to defend any shot and capitalize on errors. Dink with patience and you will outlast your opponent as he will make an error first.

Please don't mistake this to mean that strength, power, mobility, and quickness have no importance in pickleball. It's nearly impossible to compete at the 5.0 skill level in pickleball without having speed, mobility, and put-away power in addition to great technique and strategy.

Another aspect of pickleball is the extreme social nature of the game compared to tennis. In doubles tennis, you stick with your partner and your opponent with his or her partner through the duration of a match that can last hours. In pickleball, a game usually lasts 15 minutes. At the conclusion of a doubles pickleball game, you typically "mix it up" and play with a new partner. The compact court also promotes player interaction.

Pickleball can take a while to teach, and may feel at first like it's a difficult game to learn. There is a lot for the beginner to take in, what with the kitchen or non-volley zone, which is an unusual concept, then all the concepts of where to stand, where and when to move, how to keep score, how to interact with your partner. It's a good physical and mental challenge for the beginner.

Good luck.